D0351458

My Brother Kevin has Autism

30131 04124296 4

LONDON BOROUGH OF BARNET

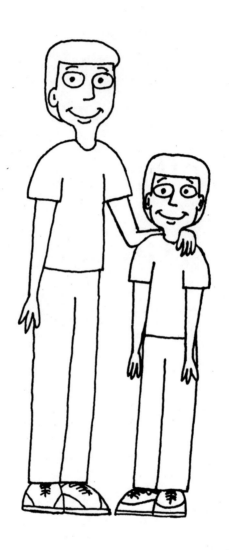

My Brother Kevin has Autism

Richard W. Carlson Jr.
Illustrated by Kevin Carlson

Writers Club Press
San Jose   New York   Lincoln   Shanghai

My Brother Kevin has Autism

All Rights Reserved © 2002 by Richard W. Carlson Jr.

No part of this book may be reproduced or transmitted in any form or by any means, graphic, electronic, or mechanical, including photocopying, recording, taping, or by any information storage retrieval system, without the permission in writing from the publisher.

Writers Club Press
an imprint of iUniverse, Inc.

For information address:
iUniverse, Inc.
5220 S. 16th St., Suite 200
Lincoln, NE 68512
www.iuniverse.com

ISBN: 0-595-22206-4

Printed in the United States of America

BARNET LIBRARIES	
23-Jan-06	PETERS

Have you heard about author, Richard W. Carlson Jr.?

Who the heck is this guy?

Find out about him and his work at:

www.HugsFeelGood.com

Kids, always get a parent's permission before going online.

FREE eBook downloads!

To my brother Kevin,
Your drawings add so much to the fun of reading my book! Thank you!

"Be grateful for the good things you have in life."

Contents

Acknowledgements

Thank you to everyone who helped make my book possible, especially my autistic brother Kevin, who drew the illustrations.

Introduction

Who is Kevin Carlson?

Kevin Carlson was born in 1978. He has a brain disorder called autism (awe-ti-zum). Kevin has three older brothers and a younger sister. Since he was a young child, he loved to draw and other artistic activities. He has always received compliments for his artwork. After graduating from high school, he was hired part-time at a store called Sage. Sage employs handicapped people who create crafts, which Sage from their store.

When I wanted Kevin to draw a picture for a particular poem, I read the poem to him and asked him to draw a picture about it. My books wouldn't be the same without his illustrations. They add to the fun of reading.

What is Autism?

Scientists have not found the cause of autism, but research is on-going. Researchers are working to find a cure and a means to prevent autism.

More boys have autism than girls. About 1 in every 500 people has autism. People who have autism show symptoms when they are one to three years old. In addition to autism, some have other handicaps as well. Autism isn't contagious and you can't get it from someone who has it.

It's important to know that not all people with autism are alike. Some are more severely affected than others. All autistic people have difficulty communicating. They have difficulty expressing themselves and understanding other people.

Some Symptoms of Autism:

Little or no eye contact

Repeating words or phrases

Prefers to be alone

Doesn't want to cuddle

Spins objects

Tantrums

Laughing and giggling when it is not appropriate

Likes having a routine and doesn't like change

Doesn't play like other children

Uses gestures and pointing instead of speaking to express wants

Flicking hands

Body rocking

Reacts differently to certain sounds than normal kids

Bad parents do not cause a child to get autism. Kids with autism don't misbehave because they are disobedient.

Some autistics can attend regular school. Most kids attend special classes and need teachers who are trained to help them. Autistic adults sometimes live on their own, but many have more serious problems and always need assistance.

Some, like Kevin, have very special talents such as in art, music, math, and memory.

The Autism Society of America

www.autism-society.org

National Autistic Society (NAS)

(United Kingdom)

www.nas.org.uk

Kids, always get a parent's permission before going online.

My Brother Kevin has Autism

BECAUSE OF AUTISM, KEVIN DIDN'T LIKE TO BE HELD CLOSE

When Kevin was born I was really glad,

Another brother I had.

Mom and Dad would hold him close as parents should,

As he grew, pushing away often he would.

"Kevin shouldn't push away when him close I hold,

His family cares about him," to us mother told.

He pushed away with all his might,

To him, being held very close didn't feel right.

My Brother Kevin has Autism

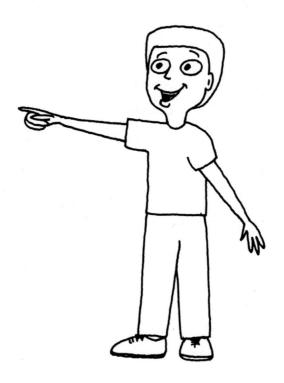

WHEN KEVIN WAS THREE

When Kevin was three,

Him talk, we wanted to hear and see.

What's taking him so long to speak?

Will he by next week?

He gets what he wants, not saying a word,

By pointing to things and making sounds he is heard.

KEVIN RODE DUKE OUR DOG

Duke, our Labrador wanted to play,

He raced and raced around our yard one day.

In the way Kevin stood,

Run under Kevin, Duke *thought* he could.

Kevin was surprised as under him Duke slide.

Away on Duke like a horse he ride!

KEVIN INVITED HIMSELF IN, AND ATE THEIR CHEEZ-PUFFS

Mother had let Kevin in our backyard to play.

It was sunny, such a nice day.

Later in the yard, Kevin she couldn't see.

Where could he be?

Mother called for him as loud as she could.

Hear her, she hoped he would.

She was scared and went door to door,

Kevin she asked about as him she looked for.

Inviting himself into a neighbor's house he had.

As she found him munching their Cheez-Puffs, she sighed feeling glad.

WE DIDN'T KNOW KEVIN HAD AUTISM

Five Kevin turned.

Talking he still hadn't learned.

He wasn't deaf we could tell.

He was able to hear us whisper, talk, and yell.

There was something wrong with him his family could see.

We were worried wondering what could it be.

MOM AND DAD FIND OUT KEVIN HAS AUTISM

Something was very wrong my parents knew.

Acting normal Kevin didn't do.

Like other children he didn't play,

He was five and words he still didn't say.

Mom and Dad heard about autism and Kevin had it, was very true.

What was our family now to do?

My Brother Kevin has Autism

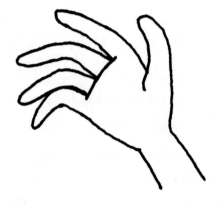

HE'S DOING WHAT WE CALL, "FLIPPING-OUT"

Kevin liked to flick his fingers in the place,

In front of his face.

This he liked to see,

Normal I'd wish he'd be.

Different he was,

Having autism, does he know he does?

KEVIN READS OUR TELEPHONE BOOK

At the supermarket, people give Kevin a strange look,

As they watch him holding our telephone book.

He has autism and does strange things.

The telephone book into the store he sometimes brings.

The book he loves to read and read.

Bring it with him into the store, does he need?

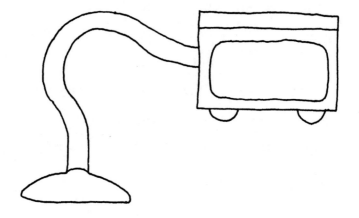

WHAT DOES THE VACUUM CLEANER SOUND LIKE TO HIM?

Once when Mom turned on the vacuum cleaner, I watched in awe,

As Kevin covered his ears in terror, I saw.

Certain sounds he doesn't like to hear,

Because of his autism, he feels fear.

Giving Kevin a warning before using the vacuum, Mom would,

It's O.K. to leave the room, she said he could.

WHAT MAKES KEVIN WANT TO HIT HIMSELF IN THE HEAD? HIS AUTISM?

When certain things happen or certain things are said,

Kevin sometimes hits himself hard in the head.

Mom asked, "Can you stop that? Relax and just try!"

"Because I feel crazy inside," he said was why.

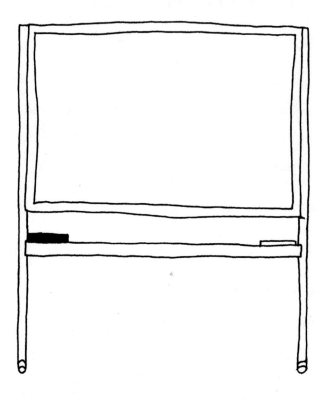

KEVIN'S CHALKBOARD

Kevin's chalkboard to him is great.

To draw on it he can't wait.

He'll draw for over an hour,

An electric pole tower.

Or copy down a section of the TV guide,

And show everyone, not try to hide.

What will he draw today?

To me I wished he'd say.

Kevin has autism, and doesn't communicate well,

If he did, to us his ideas he'd tell.

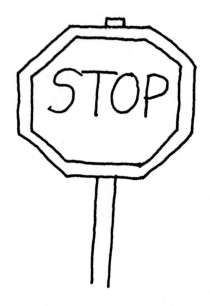

BECAUSE OF AUTISM, KEVIN WANTS TO GO THE SAME ROUTE

When in our car we go out,

Kevin likes to drive the same route.

If we go a different way,

Getting upset and sounds he'll say.

As he points in the direction we usually go,

Angry he is and wants Mom to know.

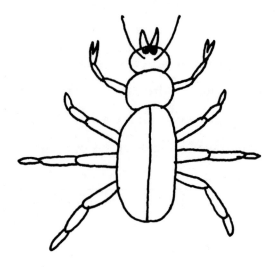

WHAT DID HE THINK ABOUT THE PALO VERDE BETTLE?

I went and found Kevin to check,

What he thought about the beetle tied around my neck.

The beetle was dead, but still an ugly thing.

I wore it tied with some old string,

Kevin was afraid and said, "No! No! No!"

He was upset and wanted me to go.

Most boys would like bugs a lot.

Because he has autism he does not.

HE ATE A FRENCH FRY OFF
SOMEONE ELSE'S PLATE!

At McDonald's, to eat Kevin couldn't wait.

A French fry off someone else's plate he ate.

Mom was surprised and looked in awe,

She couldn't believe what she saw.

She apologized and told Kevin not to take others' food again.

After you're served, eating your food you can.

KEVIN STARTED ELEMENTARY SCHOOL LATE

Kevin started school late,

He's getting older, and longer he can't wait.

He has autism and that's why,

Mom and Dad wanted to give school a try.

Keeling, is the name of the school he goes to,

Kids with disabilities go there, they do.

Mom wonders if everything at school is all right,

Having fun at school, we think he might!

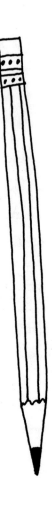

WOULD KEVIN ILLUSTRATE MY BOOK IF I WROTE ONE?

A wonderful artist, Kevin loves to draw.

He could illustrate a book, is what you'd think if his art you saw.

If time I took,

To write a book,

Be the illustrator he could,

He's talented and want him to I would!

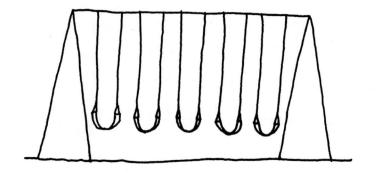

ALONE ON OUR SWING SET

On our swing set, Kevin would swing alone.

Friends his age I wished he'd known.

Did he feel bad not having others with to play?

He has autism and likes being by himself, Mom would say.

He has autism and isn't like other kids we know.

Alone on the swing set he liked to go.

WHAT DOES THE SMOKE ALARM MAKE KEVIN DO BECAUSE OF HIS AUTISM?

In our home is a new smoke alarm.

Dad tested it to see if it would warn us from harm.

Kevin heard the alarm buzz.

Berserk now he was!

Out of the house he darted covering his ears.

We then knew, terrified he feels when that sounds he hears.

My Brother Kevin has Autism

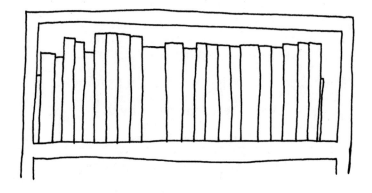

READING

In life, it's important to be able to read.

Learning how to, Kevin will need.

Because of his autism, will he be able to?

If not, having to get a job someday, what will he do?

Kevin has a remarkable memory and can often tell,

The day things happened years ago very well.

A children's book, he struggles to read every page,

He has to catch up to the kids his age.

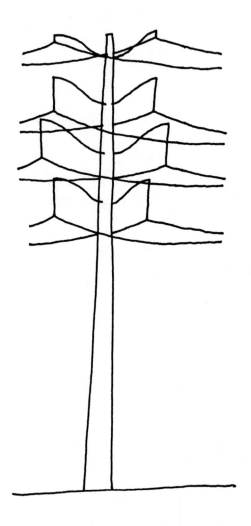

MY BROTHER DOESN'T LIKE BUILDING MODEL CARS

Kevin likes electric poles, not building a model car,
He makes them with Lego blocks, just as they really are.
He's as happy as could be,
When new poles he's able to see.
Other people might think he's strange, I'm sure it's true,
People with autism often have unusual tastes, they do.

WHAT DID KEVIN THINK ABOUT THE BOARD GAME, OPERATION?

Our *Operation* board game from the closet out I took,

I wanted Kevin to take a look.

He has autism and I thought he might think the game fun.

As he saw what it was, away he run!

Into the other room he hid,

The game he wanted me to get rid.

Kevin didn't like the sounds and red light.

Sounding much different to him than you it might!

My Brother Kevin has Autism

KEVIN'S AIDE MRS. POST, AT DONALDSON ELEMENTARY SCHOOL

Kevin is going to continue elementary school someplace new,

Helping him, his new aide will do.

Kevin likes Mrs. Post; she wants him to pass.

She's a big help for Kevin during class.

They became good friends right away.

Mrs. Post is a friend, to us Kevin say.

My Brother Kevin has Autism

KIDS TEASE THE ONE WHO IS VERY DIFFERENT

Kevin was upset after school one day.

To Mom and us, the reason why he wouldn't say.

We asked to tell us please,

He told us, him, the kids like to tease.

I couldn't help feeling bad.

Because of the handicapped brother I had.

How could teasing someone,

Like Kevin be fun?

My Brother Kevin has Autism

KEVIN GETS ATTENTION

Because Kevin has autism, he gets much attention from
Mom and Dad.

Suzanne can get jealous and her autistic brother, wish she had not had.

Give your little sister praise too,

Mom told us to do.

Important, people need to feel.

Her eyes show her jealousy is very real.

KEVIN HAS AN UNUSUAL FEAR OF STARFISH BECAUSE HE HAS AUTISM

Kevin's wish,

Is to stay far away from starfish!

Them he won't go near,

For some reason, starfish he fear.

They look friendly to me.

Is there something I don't see?

Once he tilted his head away from one, only a peek he took.

Kevin doesn't like how they look!

He eventually overcame his fear of starfish.

Then owning his own was his wish.

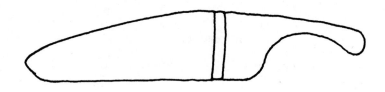

KEVIN DOESN'T LIKE THE DUSTBUSTER

Kevin has autism and doesn't like the sound the Dustbuster makes.

To clean a mess, it out for someone else to use he takes.

He came up with a new trick today.

Now he can use the Dustbuster, but in a different way.

So the device he won't hear,

Put left finger in left ear.

Right hand holds Dustbuster against carpet or rug,

Put shoulder over other ear snug.

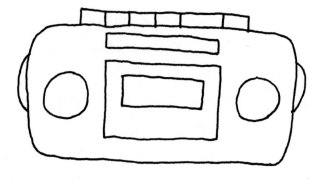

SECRET TAPE RECORDER

I secretly recorded Kevin's voice on my new tape recorder one night.

Like to listen, I thought he might.

He made a funny face as he heard,

What he had just said, word for word.

He doesn't want me to record him on tape again.

When he's not speaking, he says I can.

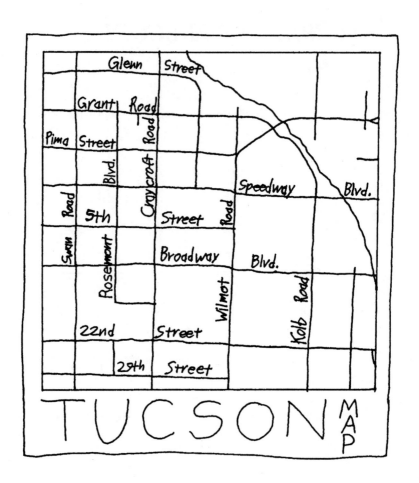

THE CITY OF TUCSON, RIGHT IN OUR BACKYARD

Kevin draws roads in the dirt with a stick from a tree.

He's happy I can see.

Clothespins into the ground he pound,

With the hammer from the storage he found.

Like electric poles the pins are,

On the road he doesn't play with not even one Matchbox car.

He gets ideas on the way to places in town, is when.

At the city he looks at again and again and again.

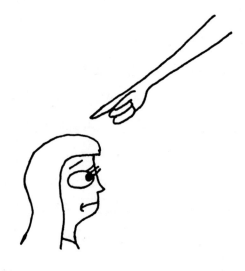

IT'S NOT FAIR

Mother and Father reprimanded Suzanne for not being good.

Sometimes misbehaving she would.

Suzanne felt sad,

Treated unfairly she thinks she had.

Her brother has autism and doesn't get in trouble as much as she.

Tattle on him she does, hoping punished he'll soon be.

My Brother Kevin has Autism

SCARY MOVIES

Kevin went into his room so he wouldn't see,
A scary movie that was on TV.
Vampires and other creatures can seem very real,
Afraid, violence makes him feel.

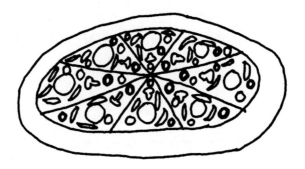

SUPREME PIZZA

Supreme pizza, Kevin once gave a taste and it was very good.

Have it every day he wished he could.

It's his favorite; when can he eat it again?

Friday, out for dinner he told mom is when!

KEVIN'S AUTISM AND COUNTING MONEY

Kevin's memory is so remarkable; it's hard to believe it's true.

Remembering when we bought a toy at a store years ago he could probably do.

I feel sad when he's puzzled and doesn't have a clue,

When counting money to buy a toy he has to do.

My Brother Kevin has Autism

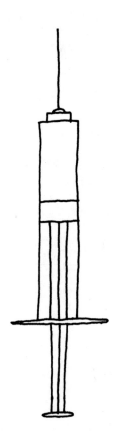

WHY AM I GOING TO THE DOCTOR?

Kevin has a fear of surgery and to the doctor he won't go.

Why he has an appointment, he wants to know.

He's worried about having an operation; is he going to?

He says he's O.K.; staying home we should do.

WHAT HAPPENED AT SCHOOL TODAY?

Kevin laughed in his room lying on his bed.

Something funny happened at school he said.

A boy mooned everyone and a teacher was told.

He was in trouble as to the office his arm the teacher hold.

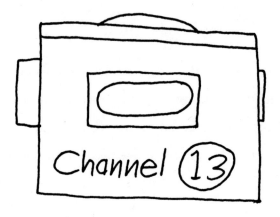

KEVIN ON TELEVISION

My family was exited when we heard Kevin was going to be,

On Channel 13 News TV.

He has talent in art, and seen on TV people thought he should,

Interview Kevin, the news team soon would.

If I ever wrote a book, I thought and knew,

Illustrate it, he would do.

A CARTOON ARTIST

Kevin knew the job he would like to have someday,

A cartoon artist, to his family he say.

Kevin can draw people and animals very well,

Creating art gives him pride I can tell.

Be a cartoon artist, he would like to.

A super job he would do!

VIRGINIA OPOSSUM

Kevin likes to draw animals on his pad.

Getting one for Christmas he had.

He draws opossum, cats, dogs, mice, and moles to name a few.

Draw any animal well he could probably do.

I think he likes opossum the best.

He drew a large picture of one hanging in a tree from its tail taking
a rest.

My Brother Kevin has Autism

KEVIN GAVE HIMSELF A HAIRCUT

Kevin came out of his room and told Mom and Dad,

Cutting his hair he had.

Dad was angry and wanted to know why.

To look like Bart Simpson he wanted to try.

Bart is a cartoon character on TV.

Like him Kevin wanted to be.

WHO TO ASK FOR DIRECTIONS IN TOWN...

When someplace new we go,

Directions we often need to know.

Where we are, which way to go, Kevin can tell.

He knows Tucson's streets very well.

Because he is autistic, some things extremely well he can do.

Directions in town like that I wish I knew!

Chilli Peppers

KEVIN'S FIRST JOB AT SAGE

Before Kevin graduated from High School in May,
Our family and him went to Sage early one day.
People with disabilities work at Sage and we wanted to see,
Happy here would Kevin be.
Making crafts and other things here would be fun,
Who was to decide? Kevin was the one.
On the drive home, Kevin said he'd like to get a job there,
Or someplace else making crafts is where.

Several of Kevin's Other Drawings

Mighty

Fluffy

Ginger

Charlie P.
Schwartzenberger

Bobby
Schwartzenberger

Fifi

Olivea
Schwartzenberger

About the Author

As a boy, Richard W. Carlson Jr. (1971-) lived in an imaginary world of his own. Today, he lives in the real world and uses his vivid imagination to write for young readers. Richard likes to write stories and poems that entertain and teach valuable lessons. He lives in Tucson, Arizona.

www.HugsFeelGood.com

Kids, always get a parent's permission before going online.

Also by
Richard W. Carlson Jr.

JEREMY GRABOWSKI'S CRAZY SUMMER IN STORMVILLE!

An out of the ordinary story about a ten-year-old boy's crazy summer!

Is Stormville a fun place to live? It sure is! It's 1978.

Ten-year-old, Jeremy Grabowski wonders if he'll make it through the summer.

Will his family move far away to Arizona? What could Jeremy do to stop them?

He has a stubborn little brother and babied sister. Julie, who lives next door, has a crush on him. She wants to be president and liberate the women of the world.

Robert, a bully in the neighborhood, thinks he's going to be a world famous movie star. He'd do anything to be world famous! All Jeremy can do is wish Robert were a dream, not real! How will Jeremy deal with someone bigger and stronger than him? He's even worse than everyone else put together!

Fortunately, Sean lives down the street and is Jeremy's friend.

Jeremy's parents are also a problem in his life.

What about the other people in the neighborhood?

Can a ten-year-old have a sixth sense and tell the future?

Maybe Jeremy will get through the summer. Maybe everyone in Jeremy's world will make him go crazy! Find out if he's taken away in a straight-jacket to the nut house!

JEREMY GRABOWSKI'S CRAZY SUMMER IN STORMVILLE!

CHAPTER 1 SOME TEN-YEAR-OLD BOYS ARE CRAZY!

How would I get through another crazy summer in our small town of Stormville? Would I go crazy and be taken away to the funny farm in a straightjacket? People could go loony at any age! Even some ten-year-old boys are nuts! Would people know I was crazy?

An unusual feeling told me something was going to happen. *But what?* A surprise or something exciting maybe? I wondered as I followed brother on the crab grass. We were going to have a picnic far in our backyard in the sun. He carried the green picnic blanket. It was hot and my blue-and-white striped shirt stuck to my sweaty and thin body. It was before noon. I shrugged and looked down as I walked.

Why did I have to have a dumb picnic with my pain-in-the-neck little brother and sister? Todd had a temper tantrum and as usual mother gave in to his wining and complaining. *Now I had to go!* Today was the first day of my summer break from the fourth grade. It was June 1978. I'd rather be at the lake on a hot day than going to brother and sister's babyish picnic. Mother and my sister, Angela were packing our food into a basket in the kitchen. Angela recently turned four years old. Todd was almost five.

"Shucks!" I said shaking my head as I followed brother. Mother had promised me the picnic would not take long. This sort-of-thing was for *babies* and not a ten-year-old like me.

Yesterday, the last day of school was not boring. A friend of mine pulled his shorts down and proudly mooned everyone. It happened in the lunchroom. Why did he show everyone his naked rump? Surprised, the girl sitting next to me accidentally spat her milk into my face. Some squirted out of her nose. Then her face turned really bright red. My friend's rear end stuck out at me as milk dripped from my face. Everyone stared at him. His pale rump shone as bright as my glow-in-the-dark Frisbee at night. Most kids chuckled as he pulled his shorts back up and darted away. I would never forget the looks on kids' faces as that happened!

Would the Yankees make it to the World Series? They won last year, in 1977. I'd rather think about baseball and being mooned than this silly picnic.

Todd put the green blanket down quickly and raced back toward the house to carry out the picnic basket. He was in a hurry to eat. As I got closer to the picnic blanket, I had an odd feeling. The feeling told me to stay far away from the blanket and go back to the house. *What bad could happen?* Puzzled, I jogged straight to the blanket and sat down. Why did I have a feeling telling me to go very far away from here?

Kevin Carlson

The Feelings and Imagination of a Barefoot Boy Still Inside My Head!
Poems and Short Stories for Boys and Girls Ages 9 to 12

The feelings, imagination, hopes, and dreams of young people revealed in poems and short stories.

If you want to have fun reading a great book, you'll find it here! This book is a collection of poems and short stories for young readers ages 9 to 12. Some of the subjects include: little brothers and sisters, parents, falling in love, boats, trucks, embarrassment, mystery, imagination, yelling too much, bicycles, cheating, wishes, and kissing. Many of the poems and short stories entertain and teach important lessons. Includes poems from the book *Jeremy Grabowski's Crazy Summer In Stormville!*

The Feelings and Imagination of a Barefoot Boy Still Inside My Head!
Poems and Short Stories for Boys and Girls Ages 9 to 12

MY BELLY BUTTON LINT

It was interesting the look on Sis's face,
When I removed lint from my belly button in a public place.
I lifted up my shirt and my stomach was bare.
My stomach could be seen everywhere.
In my belly button, my finger I slid,
And my belly button lint I rid.
Sis frowned giving me a hint,
She explained, "In the shower clean out your belly button lint!"

—Richard W. Carlson Jr. (8/19/00)

References

Autism Society of America. http://www.autism-society.org/whatisautism/autism.html#whatisautism, cited 9 January 2002. What is Autism, 2001.

Carlson, Kevin. conversations with author, Tucson, AZ., 2002.

Carlson Sr., Richard. conversations with author, Tucson, AZ., 2002.

Carlson, Suzanne. conversations with author, Tucson, AZ., 2002.

Carlson, Wanda. conversations with author, Tucson, AZ., 2002.

The Nemours Center for Children's Health Media. http://kidshealth.org/kid/health_problems/brain/autism.html, cited 9 January 2002. Kids Health for Kids, 1995-2001.

0-595-22206-4

Printed in the United Kingdom
by Lightning Source UK Ltd.
101419UKS00001B/131